Chamonix

Mont Blanc

Photography :
Yves GOEPFERT

Text :
Yvette GOEPFERT

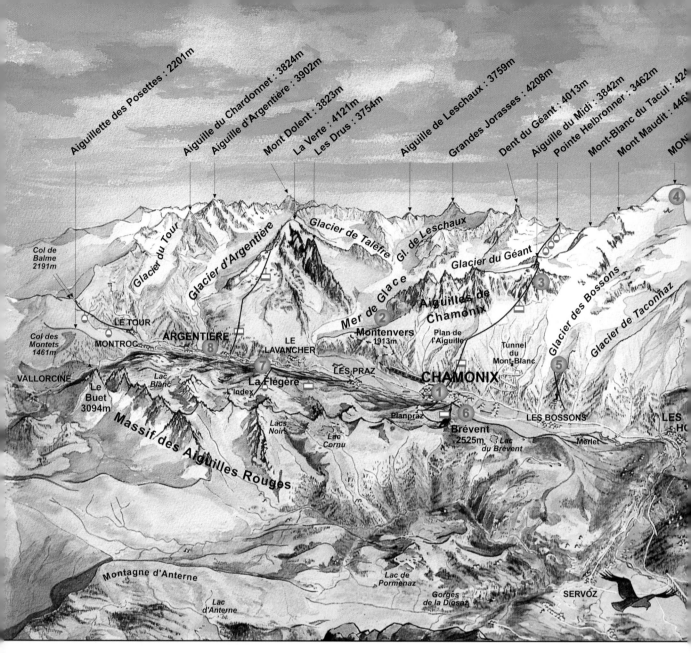

Aiguillette des Posettes : 2201m
Aiguille du Chardonnet : 3824m
Aiguille d'Argentière : 3902m
Mont Dolent : 3823m
La Verte : 4121m
Les Drus : 3754m
Aiguille de Leschaux : 3759m
Grandes Jorasses : 4208m
Dent du Géant 4013m
Aiguille du Midi : 3842m
Pointe Helbronner : 3462m
Mont-Blanc du Tacul : 424
Mont Maudit : 446
MON

Col de Balme 2191m
Glacier du Tour
Glacier d'Argentière
Glacier de Talefre
Gl. de Leschaux
Glacier du Géant
Col des Montets 1461m
LE TOUR
MONTROC
ARGENTIÈRE
LE LAVANCHER
Mer de Glace
Montenvers 1913m
Aiguilles de Chamonix
Plan de l'Aiguille
Glacier des Bossons
Glacier de Taconnaz
VALLORCINE
Le Buet 3094m
Lac Blanc
La Flégère
L'Index
LES PRAZ
Tunnel du Mont-Blanc
CHAMONIX
LES BOSSONS
LES HO
Massif des Aiguilles Rouges
Lacs Noirs
Lac Cornu
Planpraz
Brévent 2525m
Lac du Brévent
Merlet
Montagne d'Anterne
Lac d'Anterne
Lac de Pormenaz
Gorges de la Diosaz
SERVOZ

1 CHAMONIX

2 MER DE GLACE

3 AIGUILLE DU MIDI

4 MONT BLANC

5 BOSSONS GLACIER

6 LE BRÉVENT

7 LA FLÉGÈRE

8 ARGENTIÈRE

9 MONT BLANC TRAMWAY

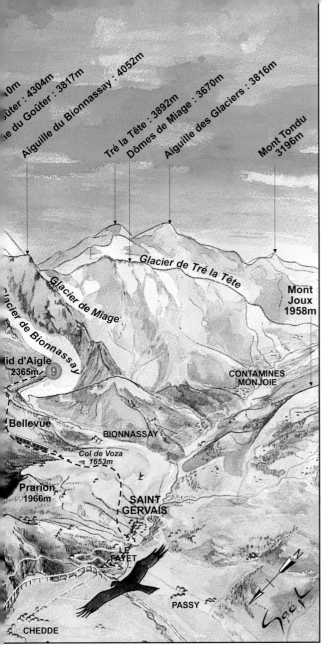

Labels on the illustration:
...0m : 4304m
...iter du Goûter : 3817m
Aiguille du Bionnassay : 4052m
Tré la Tête : 3892m
Dômes de Miage : 3670m
Aiguille des Glaciers : 3816m
Mont Tondu 3196m
Glacier de Tré la Tête
Glacier de Miage
Glacier de Bionnassay
Mont Joux 1958m
Nid d'Aigle 2365m ⑨
CONTAMINES MONJOIE
Bellevue
BIONNASSAY
Col de Voza 1653m
Prarion 1966m
SAINT GERVAIS
LE FAYET
PASSY
CHEDDE
N

COL DES MONTETS
La Verte, Les Drus and Aiguilles de Chamonix are reflected in the small lake at the Aiguilles Rouges Nature Preserve laboratory-chalet.

GENTIANELLA (Gentiana acaulis).

Contents:

Chamonix
over the centuries

Chamonix, the cradle of alpinism, glaciology and skiing, is a truly extraordinary place where technology and pastoralism, contemplation and wild passion, art and science go hand in hand...

Nowhere else is there such a diversity of peaks, domes, needles, pyramids, mounts and glaciers, or such a succession of prairies, forests, grassland, sheer rock, ice and everlasting snow...

In this unique site, human passions, sublimated by Mont Blanc, have converted this former Priory (*Le Prieuré*) into one of the world's most renowned resorts.

PURPLE COLUMBINE (a poisonous plant)
This delicate, intense violet-blue flower has oval sepals and spur-like petals surrounding its bright yellow stamina.

CHAMONIX, WORLD SKI CAPITAL
One century after the conquest of Mont Blanc, people began skiing in the snowfields of Chamonix. Thanks to Dr Michel Payot this sport, practised for centuries in the Nordic countries, developed rapidly in Chamonix. Through his example and his enthusiasm in organizing the first winter tourist excursions, Dr Payot was the true promoter of skiing in all of France, the beginning of a fabulous story...

A valley...

The valley of Chamonix stretches over 23km, from Col de Balme to Col de Voza. It is typical of the U-shaped valleys formed by glaciers in the Quaternary Era. The last glaciation occurred some ten thousand years ago. Then, glaciers covered an area twice the size of Europe; the present site of Chamonix was buried under at least 1000m of ice.

1867: The valley opens up

For a long time, the former glacial rock sill closing the valley kept out all but the hardiest intruders. All that changed in 1860, when Napoleon III and Empress Eugénie came to visit the province of Savoy, just become part of France. The Emperor promised to improve access here. He may have been encouraged in this by the

MONT BLANC, DISCREETLY VISIBLE
From Chamonix, Mont Blanc really seems quite modest: many confuse it with Dôme du Goûter. It is right in the centre of this photograph, preceded by Les Bosses, above Les Bossons Glacier; to its right, Dôme and Aiguille du Goûter and to the left, Mont Maudit, Mont Blanc du Tacul and Aiguille du Midi, with its easily recognizable facilities.

bad weather than preceded his visit: "ten strong men" had to help carry the carriages through the most severely devastated spots. Only 7 years later, an ever-increasing flow of travellers were brought to Chamonix in large stagecoaches.

This provided a constant source of entertainment: one of the favourite pastimes was to watch fine ladies climb in their wide crinolines... The people of Chamonix (or Chamoniards) dubbed this charming, if comical scene, 'rising balloons.'

AUGUST 8, 1786:
FIRST ASCENT OF MONT BLANC
Two men from Chamonix, Dr Michel Gabriel Paccard and Jacques Balmat, a gem collector, were the first to accomplish this feat. It would radically change the village's peaceful life and draw further attention to Europe's tallest peak. This memorable day saw the birth of a discipline that has since extended far beyond the Alps. Today, the term 'alpinism' means mountain-climbing, or mountaineering, anywhere in the world.

The new berlins, with their postillions in broad braid-trimmed hats, became part of everyday life. Some companies boasted bright colours and such evocative names as 'Les Express inversables' (the Unspillable Express)! Chamonix had come a long way since the time of the carts ('char-à-bancs') with their uncomfortable planks and the narrow bridges that required dismantling vehicles and carrying them on foot.

AU DOCTEUR MICHEL GABRIEL PACCARD
VAINQUEUR DU MONT-BLANC
AVEC JACQUES BALMAT
8 AOUT 1786
CHAMONIX ET SES AMIS RECONNAISSANTS
SOUSCRIPTION BICENTENAIRE 1986

A former Priory...

The name Chamonix first appears in the year 1091, on a parchment bearing the seal of Aimon:

"In the name of the Holy Indivisible Trinity, I, Aimon, Count of Genevois, and Gérold, my son, donate and grant to the Lord our Saviour and to the Archangel Saint Michael in Cluse, all of Chamonix with its dependencies, from the water called Diosa and the rock called Blanc to Les Balmes..."

This donation was made to the Monastery of Saint-Michel-de-la-Cluse. The monks had settled on the right bank of the Arve river, cleared the best situated lands, set up a farm at La Mollard and the first mill at Les Praz. Thus began the story of the Priory of Chamonix, which, attached to the Chapter of Sallanches in 1520, would last another 695 years.

The valley's rigorous conditions and isolation limited expansion of the village, which retained its name of '*Le Prieuré.*' It was no more than a cluster of small houses lining a narrow path, marked by the axles of carts. A single bridge crossed the Arve river to the pastures of '*l'envers*' (the opposite slope).

THE CHURCH OF CHAMONIX
Only the church tower escaped excessive damage in the terrible fire of 1522 that destroyed the priory, presbytery, church and houses of Chamonix. Saved from the flames again in 1758, its spire was torn down during the French Revolution. In 1807, the people finished rebuilding it - thanks to corvées and voluntary contributions - and the tower could once more raise its elegant bulb-shaped dome, facing Mont Blanc.

JACQUES BALMAT, DIT MONT-BLANC
A solitary man and genuine mountaineer, Balmat would go off into the mountains for several days at a time in search of fine crystals. His ascent to the summit of Mont Blanc brought him fame and many honours; the King of Sardinia granted him the right to add 'dit Mont-Blanc' to his name.

LA MAISON DE LA MONTAGNE
Since 1973, the former presbytery has housed the Guides' Office (Bureau des Guides and Office de la Haute Montagne) and the National Weather Bureau. This attractive building still preserves parts of the fortified 12th-century Priory.

Misery was a part of everyday life, but the people were full of courage and thus able to survive. Stockbreeding made up for the meagre harvest - a few cereals, fava beans and root crops for food, hemp and flax for textiles - and although there was no lack of wood, the glaciers tumbling down from the 'accursed mountains' regularly brought their share of misfortune. Not surprisingly, this rugged land shaped the character of its people in its own image...

And what a character they had! Vengeful, insubordinate, constantly claiming their rights, the Chamoniards were apparently prone to rebellion. The annals are full of major trials. On April 18, 1536, they refused to pay the tithe (a church tax) and so were threatened with excommunication. Granted a reprieve for Easter, they started all over again once they had accomplished this religious duty.

For two centuries, they resisted and remonstrated against all jurisdiction... all the way to the Papacy. In 1660, Pope Alexander VII granted them 'moderation' of the tithe. In 1735, they addressed a petition to the King requesting total exemption from the *taille* (a Royal tax). The negotiations, interrupted by the Spanish occupation during the

THE ARVE BRIDGE:
In the 18th century, Chamonix was still no more than a group of cottages huddled on the right bank of the Arve river. Today, the houses have crossed the river and a wide bridge, decorated with flowers, replaces the little wooden bridge, regularly carried off by floods.

War of Austrian Succession, were completed in 1757 and the Chamoniards bought back part of their taxes for 30,000 pounds: the first decisive step towards their emancipation. Finally, thanks to King Charles-Emmanuel III's liberal-mindedness, the people of Chamonix were able to free themselves of their last charges, in exchange for 58,000 pounds. It is said they 'deposited' this money, in small coins carried on muleback, in the courtyard of the collegiate church of Sallanches. This was the last time the Chamoniards would have to thumb their noses at the ecclesiastic dignitaries. Since then, the parish death registre reads: "On October 30, 1786, the Priory of Chamonix expired at midnight and was interred the next day..." Thus, three years before France, the people of the valley had their Revolution.

A little history

Savoy, the strategically located 'Gateway to the Alps,' has had a long history of successive occupations and peace treaties.

In the 16th century, after a period of French domination, Duke Emmanuel Philibert moved his capital from Chambéry to Turin: more or less definitive boundaries were set by the Treaty of Lyons in 1602.

In 1713, after the War of Spanish Succession, the Treaty of Utrecht restored Savoy to Victor Amédée who also became King of Sicily. Five years later, he lost this title in exchange for the Kingdom of Sardinia.

In 1742, during the War of Austrian Succession, Savoy was occupied by Spanish troops, but the treaty of Aix-la-Chapelle in 1748 restored it once again to King Charles Emmanuel III.

In 1792, the French Revolutionary armies of General Montesquiou occupied the province; it became French according to the will of the people.

The Directoire followed the Convention, and Bonaparte defeated the Sardinian army: with the 1796 treaty of Paris, Savoy was withdrawn from Victor Amédée III, and divided into two French *départements*: Mont Blanc and Léman. After Napoleon was routed, Victor Emmanuel I was again in possession of his Kingdom of Sardinia, including Savoy (treaties of Paris of 1814 and 1815).

Finally, in 1858, Napoleon III and Cavour agreed that, in exchange for French support against the Austrian occupation, Italy would cede Savoy and the Comté de Nice, with the consent of their respective populations. On April 4, 1860, the people of Savoy voted resoundingly in favour of becoming French: 130,533 yes votes against 235 no votes. The province was then divided into the two *départements* of Savoie and Haute-Savoie

and Man...

Chamonix owes its amazing destiny to the enthusiasm of a few men.

1741: Windham and Pococke

That year, two Englishmen unknowingly launched the modest little village's prodigious ascension. The first was Richard Pococke, a famous explorer known for his travel accounts of Egypt, Arabia, Asia, Turkey... The second, Windham, at 24 was preparing for a career in the military. With some friends, these two Englishmen planned to see those distant mountains visible from Geneva. At the time, the valley had a bad reputation and the inaccessible wilderness of the mountains made them 'accursed.'

RUE JOSEPH-VALLOT
In August 1890, Joseph Vallot realized his wild ambition to set up an observatory for studying high-altitude phenomena, 300m from the summit of Mont Blanc.

1. Aig. de Saussure
2. Rochers Rouges
3. Mont-Blanc
4. Les Bosses
   (Observatoire Vallot)
5. Dôme du Goûter
6. Aig. du Goûter
7. Glacier des Bossons
8. Glacier de Taconnaz
9. Montagne de la Côte
10. Refuge des Grands Mulets

CENTRE SPORTIF DE CHAMONIX
The spacious sports and school complex of Chamonix is superbly located, in full view of Mont Blanc. In addition to many outdoor fields and indoor rooms, it comprises a library and the national school for skiing and alpinism, a 50m outdoor swimming pool with diving board and a 25m indoor pool with a popular water chute.

These amateurs of 'Glacières' left Geneva well prepared. On the third day, they reached a 'pleasant valley' where they were greeted by 'a kind old man, the local prior.' He plied them with polite remarks but discouraged them from climbing further. Little did he know the mettle of these hardy explorers on their way to the first expedition to Montenvers.

Le Prieuré's inhabitants were far from expecting the repercussions of this first ascent. They had other worries: Spanish troops were threatening

---

WINTER SCENES
When winter spreads its great white mantle, everything seems soft and sparkling.
Nestled in its valley, Chamonix is like a city of the gods, preparing its fireside evenings in secret. Is it to recall Dr Payot trekking to the hamlets with planks on his feet? or the headlines on the first Olympic games in 1924, and the lovely ladies in skirts and fur-lined hats, and gentlemen with carefully trimmed mustaches... cravatted athletes on bobsleighs... curling... hockey?

to occupy all of Savoy. Things would happen very quickly, however, and the Savoyard *glacières* were already invading Genevan salons...

1760: Horace-Bénédict de Saussure
A few years later, this young Genevan naturalist, only twenty, left alone on foot to visit the glaciers of 'Chamouni.' As soon as he arrived, he went to Montenvers and climbed to the summit of Le Brévent where he could easily observe and admire Mont Blanc. Realizing the scientific value of this summit, towering above all the others, he offered a rich reward to the first person to find the way up... It would take another 26 years before any attempt was successful.

August 8, 1786: Paccard and Balmat
Michel-Gabriel Paccard was born in Chamonix. He early showed a pronounced taste for the natural sciences and loved to roam the mountains. He studied medicine and became the region's first physician. His patients included the wife and daughter of Jacques Balmat, whose sister he married ten years after the famous ascent.

Jacques Balmat, a professional gem collector, had an innate feel for the mountains. A withdrawn, secretive man, he was disliked by the guides who saw him as a major competitor.

Paccard and Balmat knew each other well and were complementary. Both were driven by the same will to find a route to the summit of Mont Blanc. They departed in the afternoon of August 7, bivouacked at the top of Montagne de la Côte and left again at 4am the next day. Each movement was followed by telescope from Chamonix and, on August 8, 1786, at 6:23pm, the two men reached the top together. The way was open at last...

Bad weather would hound poor Saussure, who had to wait yet another year before seeing the top of the Alps for himself.

Saussure's ascent

The heavily laden caravan left Chamonix on August 1, 1787. Eighteen guides, including Jacques Balmat, were needed to carry the heavy scientific equipment. In addition to the supplies, Saussure had brought along such personal possessions as a parasol, a tent, a folding bed, a mattress, sheets, blankets; two frock coats, three jackets, three waistcoats, six shirts, a travel suit, a white suit; boots, gaiters, a pair of long-pointed shoes, two pair of short-pointed shoes and even... a pair of slippers! He certainly enjoyed his comfort.

At the end of three days of laborious effort, this first scientific expedition reached its goal. It would be a model for all the others.

Saussure was the first to have discovered the major laws of glaciology. He developed such measuring instruments as the hair hygrometer. His accounts and observations describing the techniques used by the pioneers of alpinism had considerable repercussions at the time, and remain of great value even today.

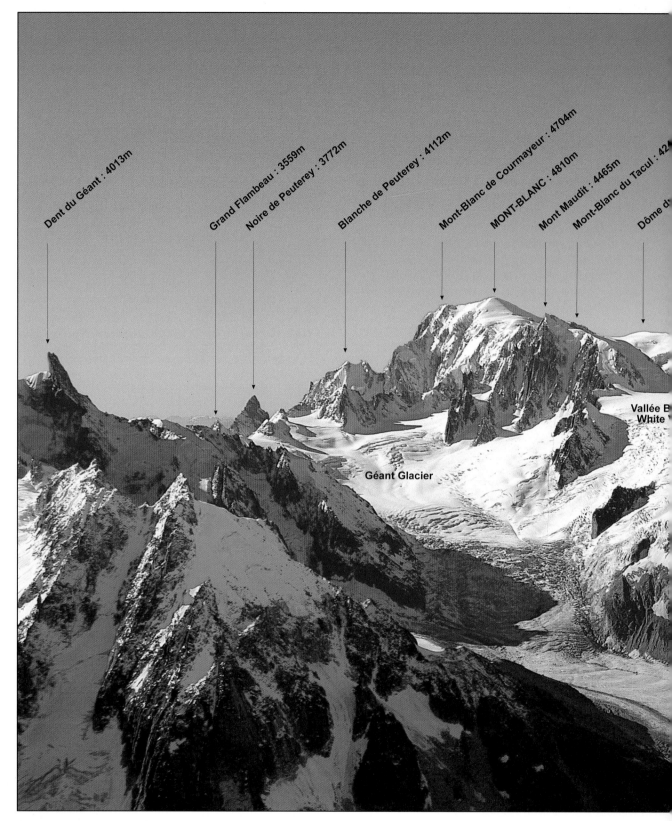

Dent du Géant : 4013m
Grand Flambeau : 3559m
Noire de Peuterey : 3772m
Blanche de Peuterey : 4112m
Mont-Blanc de Courmayeur : 4704m
MONT-BLANC : 4810m
Mont Maudit : 4465m
Mont-Blanc du Tacul : 42
Dôme d

Vallée B
White

Géant Glacier

1808-1838:
the first women on the mountain

Marie Paradis's was a laborious ascent... The guides had convinced her: "You are a good girl, you need to win. Come with us; the foreigners will want to see you and will be generous with you." So off she went, dragged, carried, pulled, half dead by the time she reached the top.

Thirty years later, it was Henriette d'Angeville's turn. This intrepid young woman meticulously prepared her expedition. Her ascent won her the admiration of her guides who called her the 'Mont Blanc's fiancee.'

The attraction of Mont Blanc would long over-shadow any interest in the neighbouring summits.

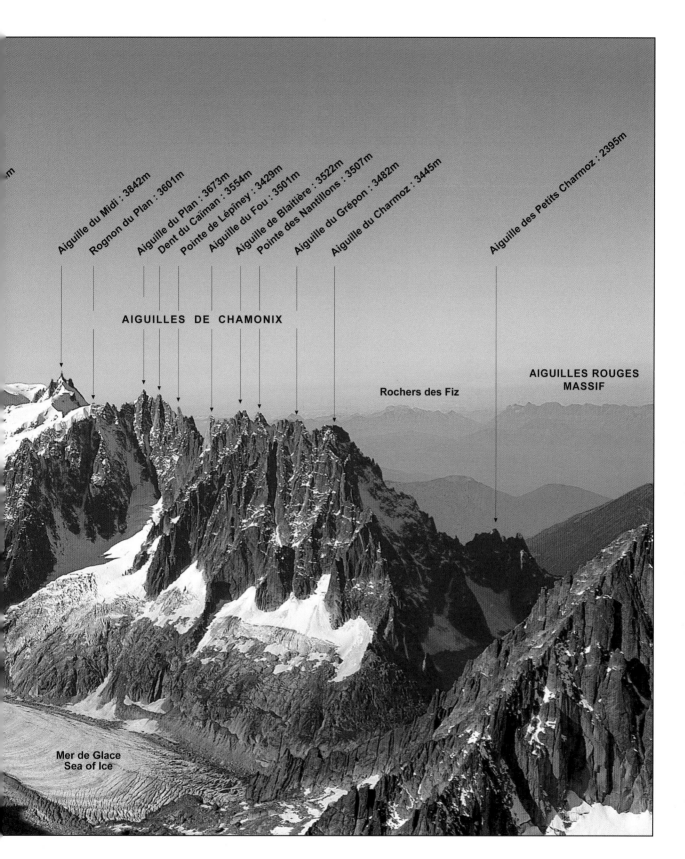

Aiguille du Midi : 3842m
Rognon du Plan : 3601m
Aiguille du Plan : 3673m
Dent du Caïman : 3554m
Pointe de Lépiney : 3429m
Aiguille du Fou : 3501m
Aiguille de Blaitière : 3522m
Pointe des Nantillons : 3507m
Aiguille du Grépon : 3482m
Aiguille du Charmoz : 3445m
Aiguille des Petits Charmoz : 2395m

AIGUILLES DE CHAMONIX

Rochers des Fiz

AIGUILLES ROUGES MASSIF

Mer de Glace
Sea of Ice

By 1860, Whymper would distinguish himself by scaling many of them: Aiguille d'Argentière, Tré-la-Tête, Mont Dolent, La Verte, one of the peaks in the Grandes Jorasses and, finally, the Matterhorn. A few years later, Mummery would launch a new style: acrobatic alpinism.

THE MONT BLANC MASSIF
Mont Blanc is not just the tallest mountain in the Alps, it is also a massif with a thousand facets, stretching over fifty kilometres, with a maximum width of fifteen kilometers. Everlasting ice and snow alone cover approx. 120km².

La Mer de Glace and Montenvers

La Mer de Glace (Sea of Ice) is the largest glacier in France. From its source on Plateau du Géant to its tongue, it stretches over more than 11 kilometres with a 3000m change in altitude.

The site of Montenvers affords a wonderful panorama of its final meanders at the foot of Le Dru and La Verte, with the Grandes Jorasses in the background.

RUSTY ALPENROSE
This rhododendron thrives on the slopes of Montenvers. In summer it is covered with rosy-red bell-shaped flowers.

LA MER DE GLACE
The once 'accursed' glacier is now one of the most popular curiosities in the world. It can be approached in several ways: from the comfort of the panoramic terrace; by visiting the Ice Grotto, skillfully carved anew each year; or in more athletic fashion, skiing down the famous Vallée Blanche (White Valley), or trudging through the séracs.

In Windham and Pococke's footsteps

When Windham and Pococke reached Montenvers in June 1741, their view of the glacier was very different from what we see now. There were huge séracs on the site of today's train station, like congealed waves in a sea of ice (*mer de glace*). Twenty years later, Saussure compared the glacier surface to "that of a sea suddenly frozen over, not during the storm, but at the instant the wind had settled, while the waves, though still high, were blunted and rounded." The marquis de Pezay, too, was awestruck by this sight, declaiming: "Monstrous diamonds, looking from afar like a resplendent scarf on the globe; here, you offer me only horror, dread, disaster, upheaval!"
To each his description...

In 1802, the road to Montenvers was widened: visitors were offered mules, guides and sedan chairs. It was possible to cross La Mer de Glace, with the help of *rentourneurs*, young men recruited to take the pack animals back down and over to the opposite slope to meet their customers. Another flourishing activity was the sale of socks to slip over shoes, for a better grip on the ice...

In 1860, the trail was improved in preparation for the solemn visit of Napoleon III and Empress Eugénie. On that day, more than 60 guides escorted the august visitors and their brilliant court. This did not prevent the intrepid Empress from rushing onto the ice to meet 'one of the highest waves, so acute' the Emperor could not follow her...

The Montenvers train

At the end of the 19th century, Swiss promoters, following their success with the Jungfrau rack railway, offered to install one between Chamonix and La Mer de Glace. The Chamoniards and their town council fiercely opposed this plan: the fate of 300 guides and 200 mule owners was at stake. When the matter was brought before the General Council (of the *département* of Savoy), it declared State approval of the railway; the line was inaugurated in 1908.

Thenceforth, two passenger cars, simply hooked together, were backed up for the ascent, held back for the descent by a heavy locomotive at the incredible speed of 7km/h!

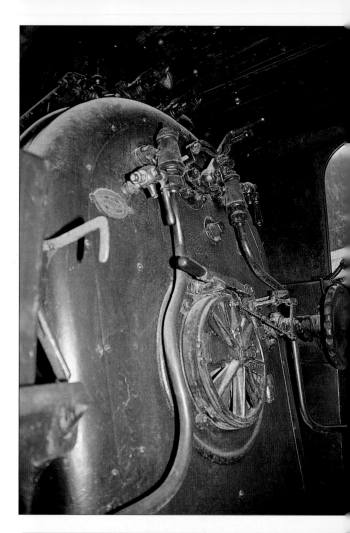

The line was 5km long for 871m change in altitude, with a 1:4 gradient.
It took 55 minutes to complete the climb, with several stops for water.

The journey through the forest offers splendid vistas over the valley and Aiguilles Rouges, Le Dru concealing Aiguille Verte behind its impressive mass. After the final S-shaped viaduct, comes the great revelation: from the terrace overlooking La Mer de Glace, the eye follows the glacier's elegant curve. According to the season, it may appear loaded with morainal debris or resplendently white under fresh snow.

Recent operation of the line in winter has opened up this refined and delicate universe of ice and crystal where Nature reigns supreme.

1	6
2	5
3	4

MONTENVERS'S FIRST STEAM LOCOMOTIVE

1. DETAILS OF THE BOILER
The boiler burned 140kg of coal per trip. Its slanting position enabled it to remain horizontal on the slopes.

2. THE LOCOMOTIVE
Each locomotive weighed 17.5T tare and 20.3T gross weight including 1800 litres of water.

3. THE NAME PLAQUE of the Swiss manufacturer, specialized in this type of equipment.

4. THE LOCOMOTIVE AS A MONUMENT
The exhaust nozzle was equipped with fume and smoke-control systems.

5. COGWHEELS AND RACK
Each locomotive was equipped with four brakes, one of which, controlled by the speed regulator, blocked the machine whenever its speed exceeded 9km/h. Rack and cogwheels were indispensable on slopes.

6. WORLD PREMIERE IN 1954
(Model in the departure station)
1954 brought a major improvement: electrification of the line. The use of a single-phase current motor for a rack railway was an international first. It made the Chemin de Fer du Montenvers one of the world's most modern rack railways at the time. Today, 200 passengers are carried at speeds ranging from 14 to 20km/h, according to the slope. The length of the trip is down to 20 minutes.

The Temple of Nature

Around 1776, a British gentleman had a crude cabin built here: Blair's hospital. A few years later, perhaps because of the poor weather he experienced, Ambassador de Semonville had planned to erect a real refuge at his expense, but unfortunately he was captured by Austrian troops. The project, taken up by Félix Desportes, was completed in 1778. This listed 'historic monument,' the oldest refuge in the Alps, has been restored by *Les Amis du Vieux Chamonix* association. In summer, it becomes an annex of the museum of Chamonix.

Hôtel du Montenvers

Today's hotel-restaurant goes back to 1879. With its exceptional panoramic view, it is the departure point for many excursions. Its predecessor could boast of having lodged the pioneers of glaciology: Forbes, Tyndall, Vallot and many others who studied La Mer de Glace in the field. No other glacier has yielded so many data or measurements. Around 1870, in addition to old engravings and written accounts, there are studies of variations in length and speed.

GLACIER TONGUE (from Le Chapeau)
The glacier tongue, considerably reduced in size, has retreated behind Rochers des Mottets, leaving the lateral moraine apparent.

MONTENVERS STATION
Above the station, a panoramic trail leads, through a succession of hairpin turns, to Signal de Forbes (2198m) with an exceptional view over La Mer de Glace, and Les Grandes Jorasses.

LE (or les) DRU (s) is divided near the top into two 'heads,' of almost equal altitude.

1. Aiguille Carrée
2. La Verte : 4122m
3. Aiguille sans nom
4. Les Drus : 3754m
5. Flammes de Pierre
6. Glacier du Nant Blanc

Speed: 1cm/hour

Glaciers advance... This discovery was made fortuitously after incidents and accidents on the glaciers. For instance, a ladder left in the séracs of Le Géant Glacier was found more than 4km downstream 44 years later. The mean speed of La Mer de Glace was estimated at 100m/year, or 1cm/hour, but the ice slips in irregular fashion; it behaves like the stream in a river and accelerates with the slope: the speed attains 930m yearly, or 2.5m daily at the séracs.

Independently of this movement, the glacier front advances and retreats. All accounts of the glaciers of Chamonix make reference to this over the past 500 years. A glacier rises when the accumulation of snow feeding it is greater than the amount of melting snow; when the opposite is true, it subsides.

'Exorcising' La Mer de Glace

Between 1590 and 1645, a series of very cold winters led the glaciers to advance considerably, and they reached their historic maximum. La Mer de Glace, prolonged by Les Bois Glacier, almost completely blocked off the Arve valley. To combat this menace, the inhabitants asked the Bishop of Geneva to come 'exorcise' the mountains of ice, the source of all their misfortunes. The procedure seems to have been quite effective: the accursed glaciers have been retreating ever since!

Crevasses and séracs

Ice is not elastic enough to shape perfectly to the relief of the rock bed. When there is a break in the slope, it fractures transversely and the sliding effect separates it into crevasses of varying width. Once the obstacle has been cleared, the crevasses close up again. Bulging in the rock bed causes longitudinal breaks and a tortuous relief breaks up the crevasses into blocks of séracs.

Forbes' lines

La Mer de Glace carries countless rocky debris. This material, engulfed in the many séracs, appears as curved lines over 5km, from Tacul Glacier to Les Echelets. These regular marks, described by Forbes, appear on glaciers as they cross rock barriers - here, Séracs du Géant. The dark lines correspond to the virtually constant rockfalls occurring in warm periods, and the lighter lines to winter snowfall. Forbes' lines, roughly one per year, represent a natural marking system deep inside the glacier. They are shaped by the differential movement of the ice, which is slower on the sides. They make it possible to follow variations in speed over the fifty years visible on the surface.

Les Bois Glacier
(1840)

LES BOIS GLACIER, from an old engraving (1840)
At the time, La Mer de Glace was prolonged by Les Bois Glacier. It submerged Rochers des Mottets and threatened the cottages of Les Bois.

By 1850, the glacier had begun to subside; consequently, Les Bois Glacier disappeared and with it, la Grotte d'Arveyron (Arveyron Cave), a famous tourist attraction, observed for the last time in 1873.

La Mer de Glace and Vallée Blanche

Origins of La Mer de Glace

La Mer de Glace is formed by the confluence of three glaciers: **Leschaux Glacier** at the foot of Grandes Jorasses, **Géant Glacier** with Vallée Blanche and Tacul Glacier, and **Talèfre Glacier**, separated from La Mer de Glace after the strong subsidence of the fifties.

Section and thickness

Tacul

Cascades

Echelets

Montenvers

Rise and subsidence:

Major subsidence, around 1955

Last major rise, around 1850

Historic maximum, around 1645

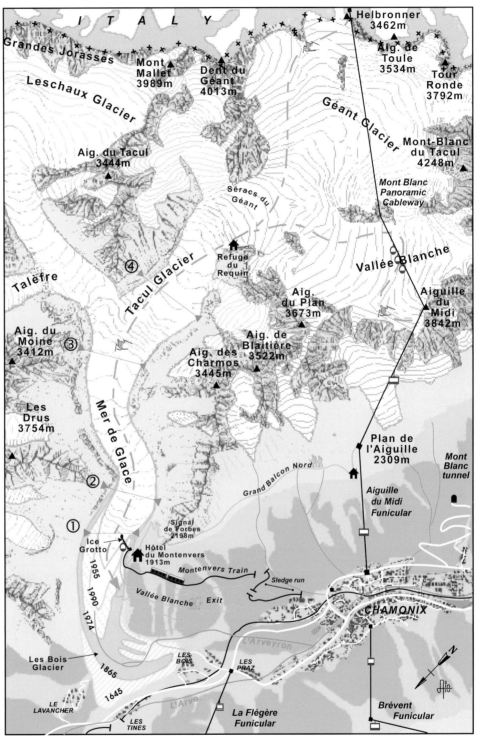

Legend:

Alpine prairie	Torrent
Rhododendron moor	Railway
Forest	Cross section
Glacier	Ski run down Vallée Blanche
Former limits of Les Bois Glacier	Path

The Ice Grotto

The grotto is a tradition that goes back to 1946. Each year, it requires four months of hard labour in cold and uncomfortable conditions to dig and carve this most unusual curiosity. First, picks and shovels are used to shape the rooms, and 800 tons of ice are removed on sledges. Then the artists' hands gradually shape the translucent bluish grotto, decorating it with furniture and accessories. It literally sparkles under the spotlights.

Ice Cave
(take warm clothing)

The easy way is to take the cable car down. But a few hairpin turns will lead the bravest hikers down to the glacier in 20 minutes. (Remember, at the beginning of the 19th century, there was ice all the way up to where the station is today!) At the intersection, take time to follow the edge of La Mer de Glace on the right to the ladders and, before visiting the Cave, look for the previous year's excavation, carried approx. 45m lower down by the glacier.

THE ICE CAVE
1. The kitchen,
2. The entrance hall,
3. Détails of the bathroom.

CROSSING LA MER DE GLACE
(from an old engraving):
At the time, visitors could hire guides and sedan chairs to cross the glacier.

Section of a valley glacier (Argentière Glacier, Les Bossons Glacier, Mer de Glace...)

At high altitudes, the snow is cold and dry (-20°C/-4°F to a depth of 10m at the summit of Mont Blanc) and surface melting quite exceptional. At around 3600m, snow builds up in large amounts in sheltered cirques and, by June, undergoes sufficient surface melting to become saturated and warm to 0°C/32°F. At this temperature, the snow develops into a névé, compacted under the weight of the successive layers. At a depth of 30m (approx. 15 years accumulation), it is transformed into impermeable ice.

The boundary with the ablation zone lies at approx. 2700m. Below this level, the bare ice appears, and more of it melts than accumulates.

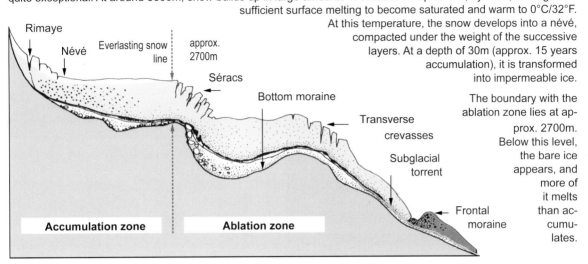

Rimaye · Névé · Everlasting snow line · approx. 2700m · Séracs · Bottom moraine · Transverse crevasses · Subglacial torrent · Frontal moraine · **Accumulation zone** · **Ablation zone**

Crystal Cave

It is a reminder of the glorious time of the *cristalliers* (gem collectors) who, with no technical means or equipment, affronted the 'accursed mountains' in search of the finest crystals. Quartz, or rock crystal is most common in the valley of Chamonix. This mineral, harder than steel and valued for its brilliance and size, is colourless at low altitudes, more or less smoky above 2400m and much darker above 3800m. Only the most practised eye can detect geodes formed some fifteen million years ago, in which it has formed in the well-defined geometric shape of hexagonal prisms with pyramidal extremities.

Museum of Alpina Fauna

Established in the former stables, the museum offers an exhibition on animal life in the Alps.

Tours around Montenvers

Full enjoyment of the unique vistas over La Mer de Glace requires at least one day. Although you may want to follow the mule trail from the start, we suggest you take the train on the way up, then walk back down.

Grand Balcon Nord (2h. 45min.)

This easy, very pleasant hike at a mean altitude of 2000m, takes you from the foot of Les Aiguilles de Chamonix to Plan de l'Aiguille at Montenvers. Follow the foot of Les Aiguilles, ignoring the downward trails to the left.

The last few hairpin curves lead up to Forbes Signal, with its extraordinary panorama over La Mer de Glace. In a half hour, you are back down at Montenvers station (Return to Chamonix by train or mule trail).

Forbes Signal

(ascent: 1h. 10min. - descent: 30min.)
Near Hotel du Montenvers, follow the path past the Temple of Nature rising rapidly above the station up to Forbes Signal. From there, the vista over La Mer de Glace and Grandes Jorasses is breathtaking. Only a few metres further the view opens on all sides for a 360° panorama.

THE "TEMPLE OF NATURE" (1778)
The oldest refuge in the Alps.

FORBES SIGNAL
In an amazing rocky environment, view overlooking La Mer de Glace dominated by Les Grandes Jorasses.

THE MULE TRAIL

This is the most famous of all, for the great names that have trodden upon it: Empresses Josephine and Marie-Louise, Napoleon III and Empress Eugénie, Goethe, Franz Liszt, French authors Alexandre Dumas père, Chateaubriand, Lamartine, George Sand, Victor Hugo, Théophile Gautier, and many others. It is easy to walk down: 1h. 45min. through a forest of larch and arolla pine, with scattered clearings, to Les Planards sledge run.

CONGENIAL MARMOTS

Just look at these chubby marmots, their agile little hands making them look almost human. Observe them upright on their hind limbs, inspecting their surroundings or nibbling on roots. But they only look tranquil; always on the alert, they are ready at all times to whistle a warning signal at the first sign of danger.

LES PLANARDS SLEDGE RUN

In summer, the ski runs are converted for sledges for the fun of big and small alike.

Aiguille du Midi
Vallée Blanche

The facilities atop Aiguille du Midi are the result of a mad wager taken early in the 20th century by the daring Italian engineer Dino Lora Totino, Count of Cervinia. This was an immense challenge: to connect Chamonix to Aiguille du Midi in two sections, one in a single span, the longest in the world even to this day.

In only six years, the highest funicular in the world was completed and inaugurated.

Since then, the cars have carried thousands of people daily to these high mountains long accessible only for a hardy few. Now, they can admire the most prestigious summits in Europe, surrounding the tallest of them all, Mont Blanc.

ALPINE SEA HOLLY, 'QUEEN OF THE ALPS'
This spiny, amethyst-blue flower is wrongly confused with the thistle, which explains its common name, blue thistle (family of the Umbelliferae).

AIGUILLE DU MIDI is one of the most popular panoramic viewpoints in the world. Accomplished mountaineers, high-altitude climbers, experienced skiers practise side by side with those paragliders of the supreme who, under the tourists' astonished gaze, make Icarus' dream come true.

Aiguille du Midi cable car: a perpetual challenge to technology

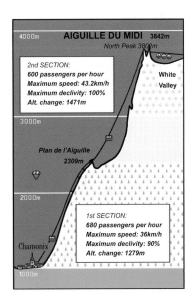

AIGUILLE DU MIDI 3842m
North Peak 3800m

4000m

2nd SECTION:
600 passengers per hour
Maximum speed: 43.2km/h
Maximum declivity: 100%
Alt. change: 1471m

White Valley

3000m

Plan de l'Aiguille 2309m

2000m

1st SECTION:
680 passengers per hour
Maximum speed: 36km/h
Maximum declivity: 90%
Alt. change: 1279m

Chamonix

1000m

RECOMMENDATIONS:

This fabulous high-mountain world lies between 1000m and 3800m in altitude; that is why this excursion is not recommended for children under the age of two, or for people with heart problems.

- **Take warm clothing**: even on a bright summer day, the temperature at the top may be only -10°C/ 14°F.

- **Don't forget sunglasses**: against the strong solar radiation and reverberation.

- **For Helbronner Point, don't forget to take compulsory identity papers.**

CHAMONIX-SUD:
THE DEPARTURE STATION
General view over Chamonix and, opposite, the ascent to Le Brévent.

THE INTERMEDIATE STATION
Plan de l'Aiguille is reached in only 8 minutes. It is most pleasant to pause here at the foot of Aiguilles de Chamonix, before going on up. This former alp (high-mountain pasture) offers a view over all the vegetation zones, from forest to scrubland, from alpine grassland to moraine and glaciers.

PANORAMA OVER
LES BOSSONS GLACIER
This glacier descends directly from Mont Blanc in successive tiers over 3600m in altitude; it is the largest icefall in Europe.

PANORAMA FROM PLAN DE L'AIGUILLE
*On the valley floor, the hamlets of Les Bossons,
Taconnaz, Les Houches, then Col de Voza and Le
Prarion. Opposite, the buttresses of Le Brévent
and its Aiguillette (little Needle); beyond, the mas-
sifs of Les Fiz and Les Aravis.*

August 1818:
First ascent of Piton Nord (3802m)

On arriving in Chamonix, the Count Malcze-
wski had a single purpose in mind, Mont Blanc.
Since Aiguille du Midi was still unconquered, the
young Pole decided to climb both Aiguille du Midi and Mont Blanc in one
expedition, a most ambitious project
at the time... From Montenvers, the
Count and his six guides went up
La Mer de Glace and camped at Le
Tacul. Then, all roped together, they
crossed a vast snowfield, reaching
Piton Nord (North Peak) without too
much hardship. They would have to
be satisfied with this first, since Mont
Blanc proved unattainable.

THE IMPRESSIVE NORTH WALL:
*A single span, the longest in the
world, hangs above the séracs and
crevasses of Pélerins Glacier, then
over the impressive North wall, which
has been scaled on all sides. On
Frendo trail, the best known, roped
parties can often be seen hard at
work. Other remarkable feats include
descent on skis or snow boards of all
the snow corridors, which in places
require rappelling!*

Scaling
rock

Grandes Jorasses
4208m

Dent du Géant
4013m

Aiguille de Toule
3534m

Tour Ro
379

PANORAMA OF THE MONT BLANC TERRACE
Emerging like a giant thumb, the Piton Sud scaling rock
(Rocher d'escalade) provides mountaineering specialists an excellent terrain for practice.
Only the jackdaws (choucas or chocards) dispute it with them.

Capucin
3838m

Mont Blanc du tacul
4248m

Mont Maudit
4465m

**Mont Blanc
4810m**

Les Bosses
4513m

Vallot Refuge
4362m

Dôme du Goûter
4304m

*The South terrace offers a unique panorama:
Mont Blanc and its cortege of prestigious summits,
all above 4000m, the immense cirque of Géant Glacier and,
in the clouds in the distance, the Italian Alps.*

August 5, 1856
Ascent of Piton Central (3854m)

This first ascent has remained memorable, so awesome was the reputation of the summit. After three vain attempts, the Count Fernand de Bouillé decided to renew his efforts. Taking ladders equipped with picks and hooks, as well as crampons and rope, he left on August 4, accompanied by ten guides. They bivouacked in Vallée Blanche (White valley) at 3800m. To fight the cold, they lit a fire which in moments sank one metre deep into the snow, providing more smoke than heat. In his account, the Count stated: "We drank a great deal and ate little..." And on went

the night, sleepless but joyous, without concern for the hardships to come.

The next day, the odyssey began:

"...Using the ladders and an axe to cut steps, we crossed precipices, but at the foot of the rock itself, there was an awful abyss...

"I sent Alexandre Dévouassoud, the bravest chamois hunter in Chamonix, off to discover the peak, along with the two Simonds, intrepid enough to withstand any danger... When they cried: 'Move on, we can get through,' we would climb as avalanches of stone fell around us... We were eleven, climbing one over the other,

MONT BLANC AND AIGUILLE DU MIDI
Seen from the sky, Mont Blanc takes on its true dimensions, dominating Aiguille du Midi in all its grandeur.

WHITE VALLEY (VALLÉE BLANCHE)
This prestigious itinerary offers an unforgettable 20km trip down the glacier. But beware, the mountains leave no room for reckless behaviour, and it requires the services of an experienced guide who knows how to avoid the dangers of out-of-bounds skiing.

AIGUILLE DU MIDI IN WINTER
When fresh snow falls on Aiguille du Midi, it adorns each cable like a garland and the footbridge seems to lead to some mysterious palace.

PITON CENTRAL
Now topped by a television relay station and a fine panoramic terrace, the summit opens the fantastic high-mountain universe to everyone. Who can forget the Count de Bouillé and his guides who first conquered the perilous Aiguille (needle), or the Count Lora Totino, whose inventiveness enables thousands of tourists to reach the most breathtaking panoramic viewpoint in the Alps in just 20 minutes.

with our hands, using sticks we handed each other... Under our feet were bottomless abysses..."

Finally, they reached the summit:
"'Stop there...' Torrents of stones and ice passed over our heads... A half hour, three quarters of an hour went by and they did not return... Finally, after an hour... they were back, pale and trembling. 'Monsieur le Comte,' said Alexandre Dévouassoud, 'your flag is flying up there, the ascent has been accomplished but not for all the riches in the world would I ever cross that ridge again... And Simond added: "My soul may go back after I die, but my body, never. Moreover, the work is done, the flag is up there..."

Indeed, the purpose of this undertaking was to plant the royal fleur-de-lis banner on the Aiguille's summit: a royalist's bold challenge to Napoleon III's Empire!

Foolhardy projects...

In 1949, Dino Lora Totino, Count of Cervinia, entered the scene. Before him, some visionary precursors had presented fanciful projects... In 1835, Eggen wanted to reach Mont Blanc from Montagne de la Côte. He planned to scrape off Taconnaz Glacier and a strip of ice all the way up to the top of Mont Blanc, and throw it all into the valley below. On the bedrock thus bared, a masonry gallery for a funicular railway would provide access "without fatigue, danger or bitter cold... to the summit of the Giant of the Alps." The glacier would eventually have covered the tunnel, thereby protecting it!

SUNSET OVER MONT BLANC

*"Mont Blanc is the monarch
of mountains;
They crowned him long ago
On a throne of rocks, in a robe
of clouds,
With a diadem of snow."*

*Lord Byron
(Manfred, Act I, scene 1)*

**TERRACE ON THE SUMMIT:
LES GRANDES JORASSES**
*Following in the footsteps of
the greatest, many alpinists
leave from l'Aiguille to sa-
vour the incomparable joys
of mountaineering.*

ORIGINS OF LA MER DE GLACE: GÉANT GLACIER
Discovering this icy world, Horace-Bénédict de Saussure wrote:
"The soul rises, the views of the spirit seem to grow and, in the midst of this majestic silence,
one seems to hear the voice of nature."

PANORAMA FROM HELBRONNER: LA DENT DU GÉANT (Giant's Tooth)
La Dent du Géant long resisted assault; it was not until 1882 that four brothers, the Sellas and the Grahams, finally conquered this devilish peak. Another first came in 1904, with the celebration of a mass... at an altitude of 4013m, to inaugurate a statue of the Virgin Mary placed at the very top.

DEPARTURE OF THE MONT BLANC PANORAMIC CABLE-WAY

Suspended over Vallée Blanche and Géant Glacier, the journey provides some twenty minutes in the fantastic world of crevasses and séracs.

During the trip, the cabins slow down five times for picture-taking.

ACCESS TUNNEL TO VALLÉE BLANCHE
A now classic tableau of Les Grandes Jorasses: at the end of the tunnel starts the ridge leading down Vallée Blanche.

VIEW OF THE TERRACE FROM THE SUMMIT
In line with the Midi Plan ridge, a view of the series of Aiguilles (needles) de Chamonix, with Talèfre Glacier in the background.

Saturnin Fabre wanted to reach Mont Blanc by rail. He managed to attract the serious interest of several eminent personalities: Professors Duperet and Lépine, as well as Joseph Vallot, designer and director of the Mont Blanc observatory.

From Les Houches, *via* Montagne de Taconnaz, the train was to reach Aiguille du Goûter, the Vallot observatory, and finally Rochers Rouges (Red Rocks) at an altitude of 4580m.

The project had received the approval of the *Ponts et Chaussées* (Civil Engineering Department), when the town of Saint-Gervais entered the scene, with approval from the Haute-Savoie General Council for the Mont Blanc tramway. This railroad was to depart from Le Fayet to reach Aiguille du Goûter; then a tunnel and a lift would carry passengers to Mont Blanc....

In Chamonix, there was a general outcry: the people were outraged and Vallot indignant: "And now that they let us find everything, prepare it, spend for it, they would put down a barrier at our door to enrich some business dealers who learned it all from us!"

Nothing doing. Saint-Gervais won out... temporarily. The section to Col de Voza was inaugurated in 1909, the next one to Bellevue in 1911, but World War I stopped the project at Nid d'Aigle.

Vallot was most certainly disappointed! But he found yet another project: connecting Chamonix to Aiguille du Midi. It was to be built in three sections: La Paraz (1693m), Les Glaciers (2414m), Col du Midi (3555m). The work, interrupted by the two world wars, stopped in 1927 at Les Glaciers; the last part took the form of a simple service

MONT BLANC
Splendid and immaculate, Mont Blanc symbolizes Man's extreme desire to rise to ever greater heights. Its ascent entails no special problems, but does require being in excellent physical condition with proper training in high-mountain climbing: the altitude itself is the main obstacle with close to half the visitors affected by mountain sickness.

The most commonly used trail leaves from Nid d'Aigle to the refuge of Tête Rousse and the ridge and refuge of Le Goûter at 3817m. From there, an early morning departure for Dôme du Goûter then Refuge Vallot at 4362m. The final stretch includes Les Bosses (the Bumps) ridge: Grande Bosse (4513m) and Petite Bosse (4677m) before reaching the summit (4810m).

Mont Blanc has inspired many records. Thus in 1864, the first official record was a Chamonix-Mont Blanc return trip in 15h. 44min. This record is regularly broken: today it is slightly over 5 hours.

SUSPENDED OVER GÉANT GLACIER
The cable car to Helbronner Point covers five kilometres of glacier in perpetual motion. Although barely visible, the crevasses can be 70m deep (the height of a 23-storey building). In this surrealistic landscape, everlasting snow and séracs stretch at the foot of the granite peaks - here, Grand Capucin (3833m), Aiguilles du Diable (4114m) - dominated by the beauty of the snow-capped Mont Blanc (4810m), Mont Blanc de Courmayeur (4748m), Blanche de Peuterey (4107m).

cable at Col du Midi. The line was an instant success and visitors flocked there. The rest can well be imagined...

The story of the cable car

The project was entrusted to Dino Lora Totino, an Italian engineer who had just completed the cable car to the Matterhorn and Entrèves. He asserted that the old route was outdated and that everything had to be started over. There was another uproar: How could he abandon the existing installations! Moreover, it seemed impossible to reach Chamonix in just two sections, one of which would be the longest ever built in the world. It was sheer folly! No one believed him. And yet...

HELBRONNER POINT:
The Italian slope is rugged, precipitous, powerful. Brenva Glacier rolls down the mountain, tearing away tons of debris in its wake. Even Mont Blanc, recognizable with its cap of snow, loses its debonair countenance.

DESCENT TO COURMAYEUR:
The breathtaking view from Val Veni to Val Ferret plunges into Courmayeur valley all the way to the Italian Alps. Pausing at the refuge de Torino then at Le Pavillon offers a chance to enjoy the landscape. A bus line goes from La Palud to Courmayeur on the road to Val Ferret, and Chamonix via the Mont Blanc Tunnel.

HELBRONNER POINT:
The snow-covered French side is good for both winter and summer skiing. Nearby, the peaks topping 4000m - Mont Blanc du Tacul, Aiguille du Diable (Devil's Needle), Mont Maudit (Cursed Mountain) - surround Mont Blanc, sparkling in their whiteness.

The administrative authorities accepted a compromise: they were ready to grant the concession if the Count were able to extend a cable from Aiguille du Midi to Plan de l'Aiguille, without damage.

A caravan of thirty mountaineers hoisted the 1700m of cable up to the top. The men, each carrying a portion of steel cable wound on a wooden frame, were tied to one another. Burdened with this heavy load, it would take them two days to accomplish their task. The descent was most perilous... While one team manoeuvred the winch, six guides descended the North wall, surrounded by falling stones and ice, pulling the enormous cable in the void, trying to keep it from catching on the rocks. Finally, after more than nine hours of great effort, the feat was accomplished. Work could begin at last.

Since then, to everyone's delight, various facilities have been installed on the summits: panoramic terraces, fast-food restaurants, toilets, telephones and even a traditional restaurant at an altitude of 3845m.

Mont Blanc Panoramic cableway

It dawned immediately on Dino Lora Totino that the cable cars of Aiguille du Midi and Helbronner should be connected. This new challenge involved covering five kilometers of 'living' glacier, with winds often exceeding 200km/h. Gros Rognon (Big Kidney), isolated in the midst of ice, was to be the relay, but the most difficult task would be crossing over Col des Flambeaux, where there was no point of support. They adopted a novel solution, based on the same principle as for the suspension of trolley-bus cables at an intersection. This one would be gigantic: steel cables anchored at more than 300m on Grand and Petit Flambeau were strung out to support a sort of suspended pylon weighing 30T, to hold up the supporting cable. Was this a technological feat, or would it be mere fiction? The result is that, since 1958, the little red cars coast high above the glaciers, to Helbronner Point.

Mont Blanc
and its massif

Visible from Grenoble to Geneva, the 'Giant of the Alps' has always held a magnetic power of attraction. After having long been feared and mysticized, even exorcised, it would become the subject of scientific study.

With the first ascent in 1786, Saussure almost unwittingly opened the way for alpinism. He probably never expected it to be so very successful, as scientists and sportsmen from all countries and all horizons flocked to the mountain; today more than 2000 people climb to the top each year.

For those who are not driven to reach the summit, there are many possibilities for going round Mont Blanc, on foot.

PURPLE THISTLE (Photo Eric Pianfetti)
However common the plant, the thistle's capitulum remains a thing of beauty, gracile and elegant, with a crimson tubulate flower.

THE MONT BLANC MASSIF
At Le Brévent Saussure found the ideal observation point for Mont Blanc. The entire massif is visible at a glance. In a sublime harmony of rock and snow, the 'King of the Alps' generously releases its rivers of ice. Does mist gather at its foot to increase its seductive power? Or is it to keep the valley and its people at a distance?

One century after Paccard and Balmat

For Joseph Vallot, Mont Blanc had to become an observatory for scholars from all over the world. In July 1887, he succeeded in the foolhardy project of spending 3 days and 3 nights at the top, demonstrating that it was possible to live and work up there. Nothing more could stop him: the observatory was built at Les Rochers Foudroyés (Thunderstruck rocks) at 4362m above sea level... In August 1890, the structure was barely operational when visitors began to flock there. They included astrophysicist Jules Janssen who stubbornly decided to establish an observatory at the highest point on the massif, in defiance of the laws of nature he knew so well. Within a few years, the building sank into the ice.

VALLOT OBSERVATORY: The Chinese lounge
What could be more unexpected than an exotic lounge at such an altitude? Scholars and visitors, after a hectic climb, found comfort in its precious fabrics. Taken from its high-altitude location, it is now on display at the Museum of Chamonix (a must).

On August 7, 1786, Balmat and Paccard left Le Prieuré early in the afternoon and bivouacked between two rocks at the top of Montagne de la Côte.

At 4am on August 8, they started up the glacier. At 5pm, they were spotted by telescope on top of Rochers Rouges (Red Rocks) where Dr Paccard lost his hat. At 6:12pm, they attacked the final slope, reaching the top together.

The return to the bivouac by night, surrounded by deep crevasses, was a major feat. The next day, Balmat returned to Le Prieuré leading Paccard, snow-blind, by the hand.

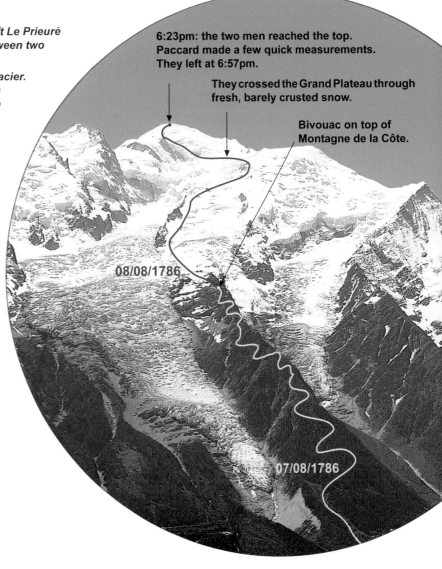

6:23pm: the two men reached the top. Paccard made a few quick measurements. They left at 6:57pm.

They crossed the Grand Plateau through fresh, barely crusted snow.

Bivouac on top of Montagne de la Côte.

08/08/1786

07/08/1786

JANSSEN OBSERVATORY:
Gustave Eiffel (the engineer who designed the famous Eiffel tower) was interested in the Janssen project and undertook the study that led in 1893 to the creation of this strange ship of the mountain... But the observatory soon sank into the ice and was abandoned in 1909.

Round Mont Blanc

Mont Blanc is not just the tallest mountain in the Alps, it is also a massif with a thousand facets, stretching over fifty kilometres, with a maximum width of fifteen kilometers. Everlasting ice and snow alone cover approx. 120km².

Circling round Mont Blanc reveals its multiple aspects and opens ever more beautiful vistas.

On foot:

160km of marked trails, at altitudes ranging from 1000 to 2700m, with many refuges.

Although it has been done in less than 22h, it is best to allow for seven to nine days to enjoy this hike with its ever-renewed charms. There is a striking contrast between the North of the massif, with its snow-capped mounts and domes, and the South flank with its barren rock and ice. The three countries sharing these splendours meet at the summit of Mont Dolent.

France, from Col de Balme to Col de la Seigne, offers prestigious viewpoints, equipped with ski lifts, which are most useful in bad weather. In summer, the Lac Blanc (White Lake) variant should not be missed. Beware of dangerous passages towards Col du Bonhomme in threatening weather or persistent snow.

Italy, with it rugged chaotic wilderness, has slopes where the glaciers literally eject their séracs. At its feet, the delicate Val Veni and Val Ferret reveal the laminated 'reverse side' of Mont Blanc and Les Grandes Jorasses. It is best to take a full day to cross the massif by cable car, above Géant Glacier and Vallée Blanche.

Switzerland is characterized by its tranquil pastures, rich in tradition. You can choose, according to the depth of snow, between Alpage de Bovine and Pas de l'Arpette, with its window open onto the ice of Trient. Col de Balme closes the Helvetian border, visible only on maps.

By road:

A 320km loop on the roads of the Petit and Grand Saint-Bernard passes.

This itinerary leaves the narrow valleys and, from a distance, presents the 'King of the Alps' at its best. Beaufortin, with its tasty cheese, has retained its pastoral character to everyone's delight. At Col des Saisies, where the Olympic Games were held, magnificent vistas are revealed from Signal de Bisanne.

At Col du Petit Saint-Bernard, open under the Second French Empire, the road gently rises more than one thousand metres above the Isère river. On the border at the pass, it opens onto the Italian slope of the Mont Blanc massif. Val d'Aosta is most appealing with its ancestral architecture, with the opportunity of visiting Courmayeur or the ancient Roman city of Aosta, famous today for its cured ham?

Col du Grand Saint-Bernard brings to mind those large dogs helping monks in their search for travellers lost in the mountains. The verdant valley of Dranse d'Entremont unveils the Swiss pastoral tradition and Martigny that of its white wine. But the finest viewpoint in Saussure's land is, without a doubt, Emosson dam with its particularly broad panorama over the 'Giant of the Alps.'

The Valley of Chamonix is reached again by Col des Montets. There, the laboratory-chalet opens to visitors the gates to Nature, to further the protection of this remarkable massif, threatened by its very prestige and success.

Round Mont Blanc

▬▬▬	Road
▬▬▬	Path
▬▬▬	Stream
▬▬▬	Railway
+ + +	International border
♠	Refuge
)(	Mountain pass

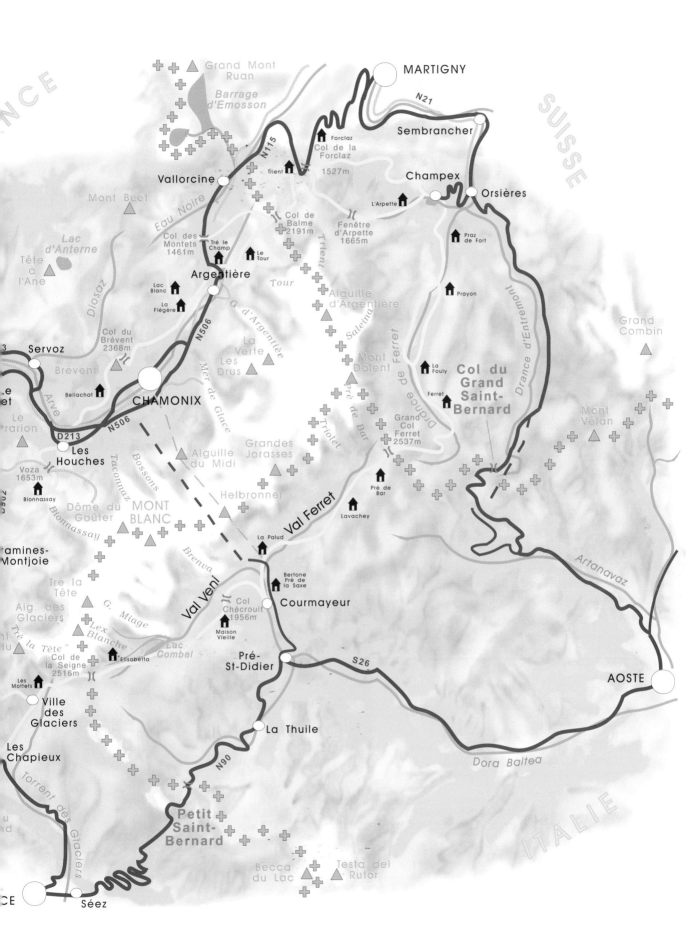

Les Bossons Glacier
Les Houches

Originating in the highest summits of the massif, Les Bossons Glacier descends a total of 3600m, which makes it the largest icefall in Europe. Advancing 1m each day, it is also one of the fastest moving.

The village of Les Houches still has some of its old farm buildings. The World Championships held here in 1937 witnessed the victory of a native son, James Couttet. They left their mark on the resort where cable cars open onto the snowfields of Bellevue and Le Prarion.

LES BOSSONS GLACIER
At the level of Chalet des Pyramides, some séracs reach a height of 40m and take on Dantesque shapes.

ROSEBAY WILLOWHERB (or Saint-Antoine's oleander) flowers brighten up shaded areas with their beautiful deep pink spikes.

LES HOUCHES: With its excellent exposure, this farming village still has some beautiful traditional farmhouses.

BELLEVUE, so aptly named, offers a lovely view over Aiguille and Glacier de Bionnassay. The site can be reached by cable car (in 6min.) from Les Houches, or by tram from Saint-Gervais.

BOSSONS GLACIER

7km long, Bossons Glacier is, of all the Alpine glaciers, the one whose margin reaches the lowest altitudes. Its terminal lobe descends as far as the forest, close to habitations (1200m). Its steep slope (about 50% on average) means it advances twice as fast as the Sea of Ice, at 180m/yr.

LES HOUCHES

The ancestral itinerary to Chamonix crossed Col de Voza and Col de la Forclaz near Le Prarion. Les Houches's hamlets developed along this road. When the national highway was built in 1867, it was abandoned, which indirectly preserved these sites, keeping them virtually intact. There are 18th-century farmhouses at Les Bouchards and Les Chavants.

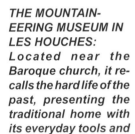

THE MOUNTAINEERING MUSEUM IN LES HOUCHES:
Located near the Baroque church, it recalls the hard life of the past, presenting the traditional home with its everyday tools and period furniture.

'LE PÈLE' (BEDROOM)
Life was made up of a succession of ceremonies from cradle to grave. On christening day, the godfather carried the newborn's cradle on his shoulder... For funeral rites, the bedroom was opened to allow the soul to escape...

'L'OUTA' (KITCHEN)
This room, with its rustic furniture, served for the evening gatherings held in various houses in turn. Family and neighbours met around the fireplace ('bourne') in the evening, the women spinning hemp or wool, the men carving wood or weaving baskets, while the young men wooed their betrothed.

Hikes around Les Bossons Glacier:

Right bank: departure from Tunnel du Mont Blanc
Chalet du Cerro (1358m): 20min. climb
Plateau des Pyramides (1800m): 1h.30 climb from Cerro
La Para-Les Glaciers (2414m): 3h.40 climb from the tunnel

Left bank: departure from the village of Le Mont
Chalet du Glacier (1410m): 30min. climb, or chair lift
Chalet des Pyramides (1895m): 1h.30 climb from the chalet
La Jonction (2589m): 2h. 20min. climb from Les Pyramides.

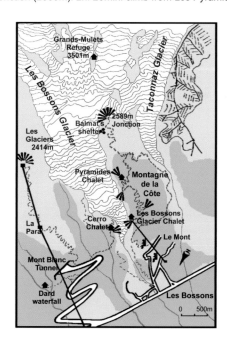

MONT BLANC MASSIF, FROM LE PRARION:
The panorama from Le Prarion, a 40-minute walk from Col de Voza, unveils a remarkable view over Les Fiz massif, Les Aravis, Aiguilles Rouges and the Mont Blanc massif whose summit is hard to distinguish from the snow-covered Dôme du Goûter. To the right, above Goûter Glacier, looms Aiguille de Bionnassay, and to the left, Mont Blanc du Tacul, preceded by Mont Maudit and its pass.

Around Les Houches

The territory of Les Houches stretches in broad tiers from Taconnaz Glacier to Col de la Forclaz, and to the other bank, from Servoz to Aiguillette du Brévent. The slopes of Le Prarion, like those of Le Béchard and Le Coupeau, beyond the Arve river, are ideal for hiking; tradition can be found at every turn in the road.

At Parc du Merlet, marvellously located opposite Mont Blanc, an area of more than 20 hectares preserves many species left to roam free. Chamois, ibex, deer, buck and marmot... share this vast area.

THE WINTER RESORT OF LES HOUCHES has remarkable snowfields, exceptionally located and varied enough for everyone's enjoyment. Beware of the celebrated famous 'green' piste, named when this designation still was reserved for expert skiers: its steep slope, or 'wall,' make it ideal for international special competition; it is not for beginners.

IBEX:
In summer, the males return to their high-altitude summer quarters, while the females, after giving birth, regroup into 'family trios:' mother, yearling and newborn. Immediately after birth, the young follow their mother everywhere and within three days a man cannot catch them.

(Photo Eric Pianfetti)

Le Brévent
La Flégère

Le Brévent, like a sentinel over Mont Blanc, offers one of the most beautiful viewpoints in the Alps: a single glance captures Aiguilles Rouges all the way to the Jura mountains and the entire Mont Blanc massif, with its seven summits towering above 4000m.

La Flégère, from Les Praz, is aligned with La Mer de Glace and reveals 14 glaciers. Its refuge is a stopover point on the circuit round Mont Blanc which, after its detour to Lac Blanc, follows the Grand Balcon Sud itinerary.

EDELWEISS, OR SILVER STAR
The edelweiss, symbol of alpine flora, is said to have originated in Siberia. It loves south-facing rocky slopes; consequently, it is rare in this massif.

LE BRÉVENT:
Saussure's favourite observatory offers an exceptionally broad panorama. Facing Mont Blanc, majestically surrounded by its cortege of peaks rising above 4000m: Mont Blanc du Tacul, Mont Maudit, Rochers Rouges, Petite Bosse, Grande Bosse and Dôme du Goûter

PANORAMA FROM LA FLÉGÈRE
Flégère overlooks La Mer de Glace, just as Le Brévent offers a unique, beautifully located observatory for Mont Blanc.

LE BRÉVENT:
The steep slopes of Le Brévent and favourable airstreams make it quite naturally a haven for hanggliding and paragliding.

Plan Praz, c. 1900

CHAMOIS:
After the spring moult ends in June, chamois acquire their lighter summer coat, with a brown stripe down the back and two dark bands from muzzle to ears. All summer, the males keep away from the herd, in virtual solitude until autumn, when the frenzy of the mating season makes them attack all rivals.

LE BRÉVENT CABLE CAR
It rises rapidly above Chamonix and the colossal imprint left by the immense glaciers of Quaternary times, when they extended as far south as Lyons.

Planpraz

The resort of Planpraz unveils a promising panorama over Mont Blanc. Located at 2000m, it is on the Grand Balcon Sud itinerary. In winter, it offers a broad network of trails which, with those of Le Brévent and La Flégère, are suitable for all hikers.

Le Brévent:
'One of the most beautiful viewpoints in the Alps'

After his trek to Le Brévent, Saussure wrote: "I was not yet accustomed to such grand spectacles... The view left me with an impression that can never be erased from my memory..."

Le Brévent:
an extraordinary playing field

The many opportunities for mountaineering, from La Brèche to Col du Brévent, open trails with such evocative names as Liaison fatale (Fatal attraction), Tombé du ciel (Fallen from the sky), Attention à la marche! (Watch the step)... with a level of difficulty rated 4 to 6 and higher.

The ski runs, from the easiest to the most challenging, can satisfy all levels of skill and the connection *via* La Parsa and Chalanon further enhances the thrill of it all.
Le Brévent is, of course, a favourite place for hiking: T.M.B., Grand Balcon Sud, passes, lakes, ridges, all superbly located... There can be no doubt about it, this is a rendez-vous with the grandiose!

Le Brévent, sentinel of Aiguilles Rouges Nature Preserve

The opposite side unveils the rocky world of Aiguilles Rouges, Rochers des Fiz, Les Aravis and, on a clear day, the Jura mountains. Aiguilles Rouges (Red Needles) Nature Preserve is a desperate attempt to protect the massif, threatened by the presence of Man. Greater awareness of the mountain environment and respect for its fauna and flora should help preserve this invaluable heritage.

Aiguille Verte
4122m

Les Drus
3754m

Aiguille du Moine
3412m

Aiguille de Talèfre
3730m

Aiguille de Leschaux
3759m

Aiguille de la République
Gra

Aiguille de Blaitière 3522m
Aiguille du fou 3501m
Dent du Caïman 3554m
Dent du Crocodille 3640m
Aiguille du Plan 3673m
Arête Midi Plan
Aiguille du Midi 3842m
Col du Midi 3532m

LE BRÉVENT CABLE CAR:
*When the clouds linger in the valley,
the Aiguilles (Needles) massif surges upward, in full view,
splendid, gigantic, almost supernatural...*

LA FLÉGÈRE IN WINTER:
La Flégère offers a pleasant skiing area facing the rising sun, accessible by chair lift and cable car, such as the famous Index cable car: fine skiing for all levels, with cross-country runs on the slopes of Aiguilles Rouges. Hotel facilities (rooms, dormitories, restaurant, bar, solarium) all facing south across from Les Drus and La Verte, provide maximum enjoyment of the site.

LAC BLANC (2352m)
Lac Blanc (White Lake) has a worldwide reputation. Deep in the heart of Aiguilles Rouges, it offers a breathtaking panorama over La Verte, Les Drus, the elegant meander of La Mer de Glace, Grandes Jorasses, Aiguilles de Chamonix and the snowy masses of Mont Blanc. The lake is very popular in summer and easily accessible (except when there is late snow) via L'Index (1h. 15min. across) or La Flégère (1h. 45min. climb). At the close of the season, it once again becomes the privileged domain of chamois and ibex.

FORMER LAC BLANC REFUGE
Partly destroyed by an avalanche, the chalet was rebuilt a few feet away, for the comfort of many hikers.

La Flégère, accessible from Les Praz by cable car

The departure station for La Flégère cable car is located near the little chapel of Les Praz, as graceful as the peak of Le Dru. Two kilometres from Chamonix, this hamlet boasts an 18-hole golf course. Plateau de La Flégère offers the celebrated view in line with La Mer de Glace, and the restful charm of the middle-mountain environment in view of the Alps' most prestigious summits. A network of easy hiking trails, including the one round Mont Blanc *via* Grand Balcon Sud, leads through the *alps* (mountain pastures) that are increasingly open to winter sports. The trails also reach the most beautiful panoramas in Aiguilles Rouges.

L'Index: 2385m

Easily reached by chair lift, L'Index de La Glière reveals the entire Mont Blanc massif, from Aiguille de la Tour to Aiguille du Goûter. The path to Lac Blanc crosses along the side of Aiguille de La Floria before going to the rocky spur on the boundary of Aiguilles Rouges Nature Preserve, and reaching the ancient glacial rock sill of Lac Blanc.

Argentière,
Le Tour, Emosson

Dominated by Argentière Glacier and the impressive Aiguille Verte, Argentière is a pleasant summer resort, great for skiing. The 2000m range of altitude has made Les Grands Montets an international success; its skiing area is renowned as one of the finest in the Alps.

The satellite resorts of Le Planet, Montroc and Le Tour extend the network of hiking trails and are open to more family-oriented skiing.

FRUIT OF
THE HERB BENNET (photo Eric Pianfetti)
The herb bennet's graceful flower develops a feathery tuft with a reddish tinge.

THE CHURCH IN ARGENTIÈRE boasts an 18th-century Piemontese altarpiece.

ARGENTIÈRE GLACIER
The subglacial waters of the Argentière and Le Tour Glaciers are carried up by a siphon to the Franco-Swiss Emosson dam, across the valley of l'Eau Noire (Black water).

UPPER ARVE VALLEY
More open and sunnier than Chamonix, the village of Argentière is a charming holiday resort.

FROM PETIT BALCON SUD connecting Argentière to Servoz, open splendid vistas over the Mont Blanc massif.

**L'ÂNE
SUR LA VERTE**
(previous page).
'L'âne' (the donkey)
is a strange cloud
that sometimes
covers Mont Blanc.
According to the
saying: "What La
Verte wants not,
Mont Blanc cannot..."
When the cloud also
tops La Verte, bad
weather is in store.

Paratrisauropus

Pachysaurichnium

Prototrisauropus

Isochirotherium

THE SITE OF EMOSSON (from La Gueulaz)
Beyond the black forests of Barbérine and Val-lorcine, formerly the haunts of bears, the view covers the massif from Trient Glacier to Aiguille du Goûter. There are two poles of attraction: La Verte surrounded by Les Courtes (Short), Les Droites (Straight) and Les Drus (Dense), and Mont Blanc, its snows reaching almost 5000m... It is a splendid, grandiose massif, risen from a Palaeozoic base lifted to such high altitudes by the gigantic forces of our constantly changing planet. It continues to rise today, gaining one millimetre each year. Here, not surprisingly, is one of the largest dinosaur sites in Europe.

The dinosaur site:

It occupies the Vieux-Emosson valley, at an altitude of 2400m, up to Col des Corbeaux (2603m). It can be reached from the right bank of the dam, up to the former reservoir. From there, it is best to follow the left bank, then up the névé towards Lac Vert (Green lake). The site is Triassic in age, the first period of the Mesozoic Era, some 230 million years old. It includes the remains of several species (perhaps 9): five-toed tracks (approx. 20cm) left by Pachysaurichnium, represented by a statue in the parking area, and Isochirotherium (a primitive reptile 5m long), and three-toed tracks left by Paratrisauropus (10cm) and the very large Prototrisauropus (30cm), which reached a height of 7m when standing on its hind legs.

Saint-Gervais
Mont Blanc Tramway

Located at the entrance to Val Montjoie, Saint-Gervais cannot be dissociated from this territory of the ancient Celtic Ceutrons, the only route between the Arve valley, the Tarentaise region and Italy.

Saint-Gervais is the French commune with the greatest change in altitude, from 576m above sea level at Le Fayet to the summit of Mont Blanc, partly in its territory. The 'King of the Alps' has made the town's reputation and the access route, opened from Saint-Gervais in 1855, is presently the most popular. With the Mont Blanc Tramway line, the hamlets of Saint-Nicolas, Le Bettex, Bionnassay and the vast Mont d'Arbois and Les Contamines skiing areas, the territory Saint-Gervais is admirably balanced and much appreciated as a summer and winter resort.

THE IBEX lives between 2700m and 3300m, where grassland yields to bare rock. The females' horns never exceed 25cm in length, while the males' can reach one metre. Apathetic and slow to recognize danger, it is incredibly surefooted; in spite of its weight (70 to 120kg), it definitely outclasses the chamois. (Photo Eric Pianfetti)

THE BIONNASSAY ALP CHALETS stretch in tiers up to Col de Voza. There, like the trees, they give way to everlasting snow. Here, Dome and Aiguille du Goûter tower above Bionnassay Glacier, and Aiguilles de Bionnassay and du Tricot.

Mont Blanc Tramway : T.M.B.

As we have seen, the Mont Blanc railway was a source of violent dispute between the people of Chamonix and Saint-Gervais. Two projects for reaching the summit of Mont Blanc were developed: one from Les Houches, sponsored by Joseph Vallot, the other from Le Fayet, prepared by Henri Duportal. In the midst of passions unleashed, Saint-Gervais won out over Vallot and Chamonix. The first rack railway on the Le Fayet line reached Col de Voza in 1909, and Bellevue and Col du Mont Lachat two years later. Slowed by technical and financial problems, work was interrupted at Nid d'Aigle with the outbreak of the First World War.

TOWARDS THE TERMINUS
From Col du Mont Lachat, the tramway enters the mineral universe of the alpine zone. Rhododendrons give way to grassland, which gradually shrinks, leaving a frankly inhospitable environment. All that remains there is lichen, a symbiotic association of fungi and algae, brightening the rocks with spots of vivid colour.

NID D'AIGLE (2372m)
The railway tracks stop dead in the middle of the ascent... True, the line was intended to continue on higher, to Aiguille du Goûter... This wild project was intended to reach the base of Mont Blanc by tunnel, then the summit by lift!

To the slow rhythm of the rack railway

At an average speed of 15km/h, it takes 1h. 15min., stops included, to cover the dozen kilometres separating Nid d'Aigle from Le Fayet. The little train's slow pace lets you enjoy the sights. Beyond the last flower-adorned dwellings of Saint-Gervais, the machine, squealing on its rack, approaches the steepest slopes along its course (with a 1:4 gradient). The thick forest, made up essentially of conifers, reveals glimpses of the valley of Les Contamines-Montjoie up to Col du Bonhomme. As it rises, the forest becomes sparser and unveils Mont Blanc's snowy buttresses. Bionnassay Glacier flows from the foot of Aiguille and Dôme du Goûter, while Aiguille de Bionnassay stands as a formidable sentinel. The view broadens as you move upward. Col de Voza approaches Le Prarion and the extraordinary panorama from its summit. There's a stop at Bellevue, a short pause at Col du Mont Lachat, and then, it's the terminus. At Nid d'Aigle, the landscape becomes chaotic and the vegetation abdicates in favour of barren rock. No more than a dozen flowering plant species grow above 4000m: the glacier crowfoot holds the record, followed by rock jasmine, saxifrage and some gentian. A path leads to the moraine, whence cascades of séracs can be observed.

Ascent of Mont Blanc

Those who are appropriately equipped can go on up to the refuges of Tête Rousse and Le Goûter. The slope is steep, rockfalls are frequent, Mont Blanc remains invisible to hikers until they reach the Dôme. But even then, it is still a long way off: Col du Dôme, Refuge Vallot, then the long ridge of Les Bosses (the Bumps), and finally the very last part of the ascent, the one that gives hikers that special feeling of achievement...

*"There can be no beautiful landscape
without a horizon of mountains."*

Chateaubriand, 1805

Mont Blanc reflected in the lake of Sallanches

English translation:
Catherine UNGAR

9 782840 470175

Editions Aio

**83, chemin de l'Olivet
06110 Le Cannet - France**

**Tél : 04.93.45.03.11
www.aio.fr**

Dépôt légal 1er trimestre 05